This book
belongs to

....

Charlie, Cara + Lucy

ISBN 978-1-5272-2477-03

A catalogue record for this book is available from the British Library.

Author: M C Duncan
Illustrator: Tegan Sharrrard

Published by TOM & TILLY LTD

BETSIE VALENTINE

AND

THE HONEYBEES

M C DUNCAN

Illustrations by TEGAN SHARRARD

TOM & TILLY LTD

Printed in the UK

About the author

Born in **Honey pot** Lane
Retired professional photographer
Beekeeper
Sing for The Alzheimer's Society – Singing for the Brain
Three wonderful sons
Two delicious grandchildren
One grumpy horse and two adorable dogs
Small apiary
Live in the heart of Buckinghamshire
Great lover of the countryside and the outside

Acknowledgments

I would like to take this opportunity to thank the following people without whom this book would never have taken flight.

My eldest son Ben, and his wife, Dee, who inadvertently gave me the name Betsie Valentine. Ernie Wise, who was the first person to proof read this book and said "I really think you have got something there." My mother-in-law, Anne, who believed in me enough to sponsor the book. Dirk Flower who one day arrived at my house with a beehive full of bees following a conversation the previous week at a dinner party – I would never have become a beekeeper if this had not happened. Sarah Peterson, my wonderful mentor, assigned to me by The Chalfont Beekeepers Society when I first joined, who still to this day, never says she is too busy to help when I call. Inez Sturgeon, who posed for all the photographs for Betsie Valentine. And finally, to Tegan Sharrard, a wonderful artist and illustrator who breathed life into my words. Thank you all.

"when one tugs at a single thing in nature, he finds it attached to the rest of the world."

(John Muir)

We harm them at our peril.

*Betsie Valentine and the Honeybees
is dedicated to Ben and Dee
without whom Betsie Valentine
would never have been born.*

CONTENTS

Chapter 1

A BUZZ IN THE AIR

"Coming!" said Betsie.

She ran out of her bedroom onto the landing and looked down at the bottom of the stairs. Sitting there, looking up at her, was her little brother Hewey. He was wearing brown and yellow hooped pyjamas which Betsie thought made him look just like a honeybee. So, Betsie stretched out her arms, swayed from side to side and ran to the top of the stairs making a loud buzzing sound.

"Hewey!" Betsie said. "Hewey… watch me!" She sat down on the top stair and called down to him again. "Are you looking at me little bee?" she said in quite a stern voice and she bumped down on to the stair below with one almighty buzz. Hewey threw his head back and giggled and the antennae on top of the hood of his pyjamas wobbled about in the air so Betsie did it again… and again… and again. She then proceeded to bump and buzz all the way down to the very last-but-one stair where she suddenly stopped and sat bolt upright in front of him. Slowly she leaned in towards him and said, "Are you looking at me?"

Hewey stayed very still, staring up at his sister, his eyes wider than saucers. Betsie sat back ever so slightly and didn't take her eyes away from his.

"Are you looking at me, little bee?" she said once more. Hewey's eyes opened wider still as he watched her. Betsie paused for a moment and closed both her eyes, then opening one to make sure she still had his full attention, she suddenly dropped down on to the last stair with the loudest buzz of all.

Hewey screamed with delight and was just on the verge of falling backwards when Mum walked past and scooped him up into her arms.

"Betsie Valentine," she said, "one of these days you'll hurt yourself bouncing down the stairs like that… now come and have some breakfast."

Chapter 2

ANNOYING MRS NOYLE

Betsie sat at the kitchen table and Mum put a bowl of steaming porridge down in front of her. It may have been summer, and the first sunny day in a long while, but she loved having porridge for breakfast.

Reaching out for the honeypot that was in the middle of the table, she dragged it right up next to her bowl. Slowly, she sank a teaspoon into the beautiful thick, golden, sticky honey and as she pulled the spoon out she twisted it round and round until the honey stopped drizzling down. Then, as quickly as she could, she held it high above her bowl and swirled it around in circles on top of the porridge, careful not to waste a single drop. Mum was always telling Betsie not to let any honey go to waste as it takes one honeybee her whole life time to make 1/12th of a teaspoon of

honey. Betsie didn't know how long a bee's lifetime was but she knew 1/12th of a teaspoon wasn't very much. *Imagine*, she thought, *working all of your life for such a small amount of honey.*

As Betsie ate her breakfast she listened to Mum and Dad discussing the plans for the day ahead. In the afternoon Mum wanted to look at her bees, as today was the first day without rain for quite some time, and she said she needed to get into the hives to check that all was well.

Just as Betsie was scraping the very last bit of porridge from her bowl there was a loud, frantic knock at the back door. Mrs Noyle, ('Annoying Noyle', Dad always called her), stormed into the kitchen, with a bright red face, looking fit to burst, holding a glass of orange juice in front of her.

"Look!" she said. "Look in there. One of your bees. I could have died if I'd drunk that juice." Mum peered into the glass and sure enough there was an insect swimming around, but it wasn't a honeybee.

"That's not a honeybee," said Mum calmly. "That's a wasp."

"Well," said Mrs Noyle, "what's the difference? It's one of yours!"

"No it isn't," Mum said. "I don't keep wasps, no one KEEPS wasps! And they are completely different to honeybees. And, for that matter, even if it were a honeybee, as I have told you on many occasions, it wouldn't necessarily be one of mine. There are lots of beekeepers in and around here, Mrs Noyle, and bees can fly a long way, they don't just pop next door!"

"Well, whatever you say," said Mrs Noyle. "I have a lot of them in my garden and I don't want them there!"

"But Mrs Noyle," Mum said, "if you didn't have bees in your garden you wouldn't have so many beautiful flowers and blossoms on your trees."

As usual, Mrs Noyle wasn't at all interested in what Mum had to say. She turned on her heels and walked towards the back door mumbling to herself about the time she was once stung by a bee, or a wasp, or something. They couldn't quite make out what she was saying as she finally disappeared out into the garden still clutching her glass of orange juice.

"Well," said Mum, "that was all very exciting so early in the day! That lady needs to learn a thing or two about the honeybees and then, perhaps she wouldn't complain so much."

Betsie stood up from the table and carried her bowl over to the sink. *Perhaps,* she thought, *I ought to learn about the honeybees too.*

Honeybee

Wasp

Bumblebee

Chapter 3

PERCHANCE TO DREAM

Betsie ran upstairs into her bedroom and pulled back her curtains. She leaned on the window sill and watched the cherry blossoms gently falling to the ground. She began to think about the honeybees. *I wonder what it would be like to be a honeybee?* she thought. *Just for a day. If a bee took a lifetime to make such a small amount of honey, how much did it make in a day? And what did they have to do that was so hard to make that honey?*

Mum told her how important bees are to the flowers, trees, people and the planet. It was the first time Betsie had really stopped to think about it. Mum loved her honeybees. In fact, Betsie's bedroom was decorated with flowers and bees and at night she liked to try and imagine the bees buzzing around the flowers and see how many she could count. That always helped her fall asleep. *Maybe*, she thought, *if I could be a bee for a day, I would learn all about them, then I would be able to tell Mrs Noyle everything I had learned and perhaps she would stop complaining about Mum's bees. And maybe she would even learn to love and appreciate the ones in her garden.*

Betsie loved the view of her garden from her bedroom window and looking at a patch of daisies on the grass she decided that this morning she would choose one of her toys and go outside and make a daisy chain, so she gathered up her teddy bears and dolls from all around her room and sat them in a circle on the floor. She looked at them all one by one.

"Oh!" said Betsie out loud, "I do hate this bit." She tipped her head to the side and for a moment looked very serious as she considered each toy in turn. "I wish I could take you all out into the garden but my arms just aren't big enough," and she stretched them out as wide as she could. "I'm going to close my eyes and spin around and the one I am pointing at when I stop is the one I will take outside with me!"

Delighted with what she thought to be a fair decision she spun around on the spot making a buzzing sound and came to a sudden halt. She opened her eyes to see which toy her finger was pointing at.

"You!" she said. "You will come into the garden and help me make a daisy chain." Betsie bent down and picked up Tid, her big brown bear, and sat him on the end of her bed while she got dressed.

Chapter 4

DAISY CHAINS

As Betsie came out of the house into the bright sunshine she looked up to see a single cloud in the blue sky that she was sure looked like a honeybee!

"Come on, Tid," said Betsie dragging him along by his paw, "let's go and find a patch of daisies." She wandered around the garden looking for a place for her and Tid to sit. After a few minutes of careful thought, she decided that they should sit underneath the shade of a beautiful weeping willow tree. The tree stood in a corner of the garden with its long slender branches hanging down to the ground.

"This is perfect," she said to Tid and sat down beside him on the grass. Leaning out in front of her she began to pick some daisies, and once she thought she had enough, she made them into a long chain, then split the chain in two and joined each one into a circle. She knelt down behind Tid and placed the first one on his head and then put the second one on hers.

"There," she said, "you can be my prince," and, turning him around, she stood up and curtsied in front of him and said, "and I will be your princess." Sweeping Tid up into her arms she ran back to the house.

Betsie sat Tid on the kitchen table and ran into the hall where Mum was going through her 'bee-box'. She pulled out her bee suit, gloves, smoker and hive tool and walked into the kitchen.

"You look beautiful, Betsie," said Mum smiling at her daughter who still had her crown of daisies on her head and then looking over at Tid she said, "Oh and you have one too, how lovely you *both* look!"

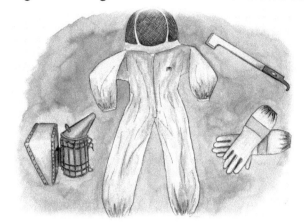

Mum put her bits from the bee-box on the table next to Tid and walked over and opened one of the cupboards.

Betsie took a chair from the kitchen table and pulled it over to the side where Mum was standing and climbed up and sat on the work surface.

"Well, young lady," Mum said, "you came in just at the right time…" Mum was looking at all the jams. "… I am just about to go and have a look at my bees," she said. "Would you like me to make you a drink and a sandwich before I put my bee suit on?"

Betsie smiled as she thought of Mum in her bee suit. She thought she looked more like an astronaut than a beekeeper!

"Can I have a honey sandwich?" she said as she jumped down from the kitchen work surface. Grabbing Tid by the paw she went outside and sat at the garden table.

A few minutes later Mum came out and put the plate with the honey sandwich, cut into triangles just as she liked it, together with a beaker of water down on the table in front of her.

"Don't forget to check the sandwich for wasps or bees before you take a bite," she said as she walked back into the house. Betsie picked up a honey sandwich and turned it around in her hand checking it for bees…

Chapter 5

ARE YOU LOOKING AT ME, LITTLE BEE?

There weren't any bees *or* wasps to be seen so Betsie popped a triangle of bread and sticky honey into her mouth. She took her beaker from the table and sat back in the chair and looked over the rim at the remaining three sandwiches.

"Well I never," she said very quietly, not moving a muscle. There, seemingly appearing from nowhere, a honeybee was standing, as bold as brass, on top of one of her sandwiches, and what is more, it appeared to be looking straight at her.

Very gently, Betsie leaned forward and put the beaker back on the table. She didn't take her eyes away from the bee for a single second. She stayed absolutely still and watched it for a moment or two longer. As she looked at the bee she thought of Hewey in his yellow and brown hooped pyjamas and smiled as she said, in the gentlest of voices, "Are you looking at me, little bee?"

The bee stared at Betsie so she asked again, "Are you looking at me, little bee?" and very gently she began to lean back in the chair.

The bee took a couple of steps backward on the sandwich. Betsie, a little startled, sat back a tiny bit more. The bee, she was now convinced, *was* staring straight back at her!

"You *are* looking at me, little bee!" said Betsie in a controlled but excited voice. Very gently she placed the fingertips of both hands on the edge of the table and raised one finger in the air and kept very still. The bee lifted one of its front legs up and it too stayed very still. Betsie's eyes nearly popped out of her head and her jaw dropped.

"Goodness!" she said and she lowered her finger back on to the table and the bee lowered its leg.

"Well I'll be," she said, not believing her eyes. "You are copying me!"

The bee turned in a circle and then made its way down the side of the sandwich to a little pool of honey that had trickled out of the side of the bread. It took a drink from the honey and returned to the top of the sandwich and walked around in another circle.

As Betsie sat with her eyes fixed on the bee she began to make up a rhyme in her head. The bee stopped and looked at her again so Betsie said the rhyme out loud.

Are you looking at me, little bee?
Are you looking at me?
My name is Betsie Valentine
And that begins with a B!

Resting her hands in her lap she went on.

Are you looking at me, little bee?
Are you looking at me?
My name is Betsie Valentine
And I'd love to be a bee!

The bee buzzed its wings and flew up into the air and hovered a little way above the sandwich and then slowly came back down again. Betsie opened her eyes really wide and the bee did it again. Betsie scratched her head and the bee lifted one of its legs and appeared to touch its head. With her mouth wide open in amazement, Betsie drew in a big breath of air and touched her head with her other hand and the bee did exactly the same with its other leg! Up went the bee again and back down it came. Betsie was sure as sure could be that this little honeybee, standing in front of her on her honey sandwich, was just as excited as she was!

Betsie sat back in her chair and closed her eyes for a brief moment thinking about what she had just seen and from out of nowhere she heard a little voice say…

"Betsie Valentine, do you really want to be a bee?

Chapter 6

A BUMP ON THE HEAD

Betsie suddenly sat up straight and opened her eyes. Placing both hands gently on the table she gradually turned her head, first to the left and then to the right, checking to see if anyone was standing either beside or behind her. Maybe, she thought, someone had heard her say her poem out loud, but there was definitely no one there. She looked at the bee and the bee looked straight back at her. Neither of them moved. Neither of them blinked. Betsie slowly began to sit back in the chair.

"Tid…" she said with her eyes firmly fixed on the bee. "Did you just ask me if I *really* wanted to be a bee?" Tid didn't move… neither did he speak.

"Hmmm," she said and flicked her eyes up at Tid. Just then she heard a polite cough…

"Uh-huc-huc-hum!"

Betsie looked back at the sandwich and the bee had gone. Quickly she pushed the chair back and looked under the table. And there was the bee, sitting on the seat of the chair directly opposite her.

"Are you looking for me, Betsie?" the bee said.

Betsie bumped her head on the table as she tried to sit up.

"Ouch!" she said. "What on… ?"

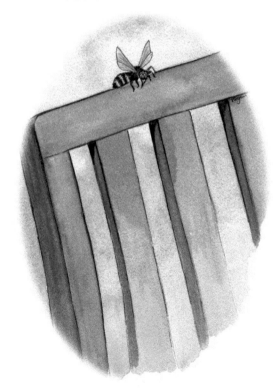

The bee flew up onto the back of the chair.

"I said," said the bee, "are you looking for me?"

"Goodness!" Betsie said, rubbing her head with her hand. "It *really* is you talking. I thought it was, but then I thought… how could a bee be talking to me?"

"Well," said the bee politely, "it is me. There's no one else here," and it looked all around, "apart from the bear, and as you have just discovered, toy bears cannot talk."

"Well no, he can't talk," said Betsie, "but then… I didn't think bees talked either!"

"They don't!" said the bee. "Not in a human sort of way." And it flew back down onto Betsie's sandwich.

"But you…" and the bee stopped, turned around in a circle to make sure no one had silently appeared or was secretly listening in.

"You made up a *magical* rhyme, Betsie Valentine, and you touched your head, and I touched mine and then something *very magical* happened!"

"Wow," said Betsie, feeling her head to see if she had a bump.

"So…" said the bee.

"So?" said Betsie.

"So… do you *really* want to be a bee?"

"Yes… yes… yes!" she said quickly "I do… *I really do*…"

Betsie leaned forward to get a closer look at the bee and said in a quiet voice, "This *really is magical* and *I really am* talking to a bee."

"Well, Betsie," said the bee, "the magic has only just begun."

"Only just begun?" Betsie said, sounding surprised.

"Look around the garden, Betsie," said the bee. Betsie looked all around her and saw lots of honeybees on all the different plants and she could hear their gentle humming in the blossoms on the trees. It was as if they were all chattering and laughing.

"Betsie," the bee said. "*Why* do you want to be a honeybee?"

"Because…" Betsie stopped for a moment and looked up at the trees and then down at the flowers.

"Because…" she said "… my mum is always talking about the bees. About how important they are and how hard they work and… and how… if there weren't any honeybees there wouldn't be any flowers or trees." Then she stopped again and looked a little sad. "Mum says that without flowers and trees there would be no fruit or vegetables to eat and so slowly we would begin to disappear and our planet would die."

The bee listened and softly said, "I didn't think people knew that!"

"So…" said Betsie, "I would like to see *exactly* what it is you bees do."

"And to do that…" said the bee, "you have to *become* a bee."

"Become a real bee?" Betsie said.

The bee buzzed up into the air and back down onto the plate.

"Yes, of course, how else can you actually learn *all about the honeybee* if you don't become one?"

Betsie took a bite from her sandwich and the bee walked down onto the plate and took another sip of honey.

"OK, Betsie," said the bee, "are you ready for an adventure you will never forget?"

Betsie wiped the very last crumbs with the back of her hand from the corners of her mouth and looked at the bee.

"Close your eyes, Betsie," said the bee, "and repeat your rhyme out loud again."

Betsie slowly sat back in the chair.

Everything looked so pretty. She looked back at the bee and began.

Are you looking at me, little bee?
Are you looking at me?
My name is Betsie Valentine
And that begins with a B!

Are you looking at me, little bee?
Are you looking at me?

Her voice grew softer…

My name is Betsie Valen…

And softer still…

…tine
and I would love to

And slowly trailed away…

… be… a…

Chapter 7

TAKE-OFF

Betsie opened her eyes.

"Hello!" said the bee eagerly.

Betsie stood absolutely still and stared at the bee. This time, however, the little bee didn't appear little anymore. They now seemed to be looking at each other… eyeball to eyeball.

"Goodness!" said Betsie. She slowly walked round in a circle until once again she was looking at the bee. "I'm standing on my honey sandwich!"

The bee buzzed up into the air with excitement and then gently landed down next to her.

"Yes you are," said the bee. Betsie turned around.

"Oh!" she said. "Oh my… am I… ?"

"A honeybee?" said the bee. "Yes, Betsie, you are… you are indeed a honeybee… and…" it said, "a very fine honeybee you are too!"

"Wow!" Betsie said, and for the first time Betsie could ever remember, she couldn't think of a single thing to say. She fluttered her wings and it felt good so she fluttered them again.

"I'm a bee… I'm a honeybee… I *really am* a honeybee!" she said, laughing.

"You'll have to beat those wings a lot harder, Betsie," said the bee, "if you want to take off. *At least* two hundred times harder. A bee beats her wings two hundred times a second!"

"*Two hundred times a second?*" The very thought of it made Betsie feel exhausted.

She closed her eyes and let out a sigh. She could never make her wings go that fast. *But now I'm a bee*, she thought, *and that's what they do.* So she shut her eyes as tight as she could and concentrated on her wings and before she knew it she was up in the air making a loud buzzing sound… just like a bee. She had never felt more excited.

Betsie gradually came back down onto the sandwich but she was too excited and went straight back up again, circled around and looked back down at the bee.

"Look, bee! Look at me!" she said. "My name is Betsie Valentine and *I'm* a honeybee!" and she started to swoop up and down.

"Be careful up there," the bee said. "Don't go anywhere without me. You have a lot to learn about being a honeybee!"

Betsie was still in the air, turning, swirling, dipping and diving. She hovered for a moment and looked down at the bee who was looking up at her and saw that it was looking a little bothered so she gently came back down and landed on the sandwich. Betsie felt as thrilled as a bee could possibly feel while standing on a sandwich filled with honey!

"Come on, Betsie," said the bee. "We need to get back to the hive. I've been gone a long time and it's quite a long way."

"Oh!" said Betsie. "Isn't your hive over there?" She looked over at her mum's hives.

"No," said the bee, "I flew a long way to find your garden with all its beautiful flowers."

"How far did you come?" Betsie said, sounding very surprised.

"Oh, about three miles," said the bee casually.

"Three miles?" said Betsie. "That's how far away my school is. I have to take the bus!"

The bee looked at Betsie, "Didn't you say your mother told you how *hard* we honeybees work?"

Betsie nodded as she thought about Mum telling Mrs Noyle that bees don't just pop next door, and was about to say something when the bee interrupted her.

"Well, flying three miles is just a *small* part of it," said the bee and it flew up, hovered in the air, looked down at Betsie and called out, "come on, Betsie, you really *do* have a lot to learn!" And with that, Betsie took off. Her wings were making a loud buzzing sound. She had never felt happier. The two of them did a loop in the air and disappeared swiftly out of sight!

Chapter 8

A BEE NAMED HUNNIE

As they went higher and higher, Betsie looked back down into her garden.

"Look, bee, at our beautiful garden," said Betsie. "All the pretty flowers. And look at the blossoms on the cherry trees, they are just like *huge* pink clouds! Oh it's *amazing* from up here!" she said, feeling elated.

The two of them swooped down together. Betsie could see her mum and dad standing in their vegetable patch. *Hewey must be sleeping*, she thought, and she wondered what he would think if he could see her flying in the air *really* buzzing like a proper bee.

All of a sudden Betsie stopped flying and hovered in the air. The bee came over and fluttered its wings next to her.

"Why have you stopped?" said the bee.

"I don't know your name," said Betsie. "You know *my* name but you haven't told me what yours is."

"That's because I don't have a name!" said the bee, as it guided Betsie down into a field full of large yellow dandelions. Together they gently landed right in the rich orange-coloured centre of one of the dandelions.

"There are far too many bees in a single hive for each and every one of us to have a name," the bee said.

"Really?" said Betsie. "I mean, how many can there be? We have about two *hundred* children in our school and *we all* have names! Some of us," she went on, "have the same name but we all look very different so it's easy to tell who is who."

"Betsie…" said the bee with a very serious look on its face, "there are about *fifty thousand bees* in our hive and we all, more or less, look the same – except for the queen of course – oh, and the drones!"

Betsie looked at the bee, "The queen and the drones? Who or what are they?"

"The queen," the bee explained, "is the most important bee in the hive and is bigger than all the other bees and is, of course, female. Then there are the drones. They are male bees and *all the other bees* in the hive, like me, are *worker bees* and we are all female!" Betsie took a step backwards.

"So you're a girl bee?" Betsie said.

"I am… I am a worker bee and *the worker bees are girls.*"

"Wow!" said Betsie. "Fifty thousand bees all looking more or less the same without names!" *That's confusing*, she thought, *and very crowded!* Betsie looked up at the sky as she tried to imagine a hive crammed with fifty thousand bees. She took another step backwards and very nearly fell off the edge of the flower.

Betsie scrambled her way back up onto the dandelion and walked into the middle, completely unaware that she was covered in a thick layer of orange dust.

"How do you all move around?"

"Oh, you'll see when we get there. We are all very busy with our different jobs but we manage OK!" said the bee. Betsie wandered around the dandelion in ever-decreasing circles, trying to take it all in.

"Fifty thousand honeybees," she said again out loud, "wow… *that's a whole lot of bees!*"
She shook her head in disbelief and *a whole lot of orange dust* fell off her body onto the dandelion. She started thinking about a name for the bee. Now she knew the bee was a girl she simply had to give her a name. She couldn't possibly think of her as *it* anymore. After all*,* she thought, the bee wasn't just any old bee, she was a very special bee and most importantly she was now Betsie's friend. How on earth could you have a friend who didn't have a name? Betsie carried on walking around, mumbling to herself while the bee stood very still watching her, wondering what on earth she was doing.

"Well…" Betsie said finally. "I think *you* should have a name… and… well… um… you are a girl… and you are a honeybee… and… and a honeybee makes… honey… so…" The bee stood quite still, her eyes fixed on Betsie. "Hunnie!" Betsie said suddenly. "I'm going to call you… *Hunnie!*"

"Hunnie!" said the bee buzzing into the air with excitement, "Hunnie. I *like it*. I really do!" And she buzzed up and down with delight, looping around in the air calling out her name and then sang out a rhyme…

I'm a little honeybee
I didn't have a name
Until my friend – Betsie Valentine – said it was a shame.
So she thought and she thought and then she thought again,
And said, "I'm going to call you Hunnie,"
So Hunnie is my name!

And with that Hunnie came back down and landed on the dandelion next to Betsie and the two of them began dancing all around the flower singing the little rhyme. When they could dance no more and could no longer sing for laughing, they came to a standstill, looked at each other and burst out laughing again.

"Hunnie!" Betsie said. "You are covered in orange dust!"

"So are you!" said Hunnie. "It's pollen!"

"*Pollen…*" said Betsie. "What's pollen?"

"Oh come on, Betsie," Hunnie said, looking at her new best friend. "Let's go and find a tree with lots of blossom and I will explain. There is so much for you to learn."

With that they swooped into the air and flew side by side. Betsie and Hunnie – Hunnie and Betsie – two new best friends positively buzzing with happiness!

Chapter 9

RAINBOW DUST

Hunnie made a nosedive towards the ground and then did a quick U-turn back up again leaving Betsie still plummeting down.

"Keep up, Betsie!" she said.

Betsie quickly turned around and shot up into the air as fast as she could, overtaking Hunnie while making a series of loops.

"Who's getting left behind now?" Betsie said to her new best friend.

"Not me!" said Hunnie as she did a loop and took off in a straight line. "Follow me, Betsie. Catch me if you can!" And off they headed into a garden with a huge horse chestnut tree.

"Down there, Betsie! We're going down there," and Hunnie headed toward the tree.

"From up here," said Betsie, trying to keep up, "the flowers on that tree look like raspberry ripple ice cream cones."

"Raspberry what?"

"Ripple…" said Betsie. "Raspberry ripple is white and pink just like those flowers… and it's delicious." Hunnie looked blankly at Betsie.

"I don't know *what* you are talking about," Hunnie said as they came down among the leaves on the tree.

Hunnie started busily collecting red dust from the blossom and packing it tightly all around her back legs. Betsie stood still and watched as she gathered up more and more. And the more she collected, the more her back legs looked like they had large baskets on them – packed full of this strange red dust.

"What *are* you doing?" Betsie said.

"I'm collecting pollen to take back to the hive," said Hunnie, busily working away. "And before you say *anything*… pollen is the *dust* that you and I were covered in when we were on the dandelion."

"But this is red dust and we were covered in orange dust," Betsie said, trying to twist around to see if she still had any left on her body.

"Yes I know," said Hunnie, "every flower has a different colour pollen. Blackberries have green, rock rose is pink, willow is yellow and so on. There are many different pollen colours."

"It sounds like a rainbow," Betsie said and began to sing the rainbow song. "*Red and yellow and pink and green, purple and orange and blue…*"

"Well yes, I suppose so," Hunnie said. "Although I can't think of any flower that has blue pollen!"

"What do you want *pollen* for?"

"It's a source of food," Hunnie said. "We feed it to the baby bees. It helps them grow and makes them strong. Without it no young bee would survive." She stopped what she was doing and went and stood beside Betsie and showed her the pollen she had packed around her back legs and the pollen that had just stuck to her head and body while she had been busy.

"The pollen in the baskets on our legs," she said, "we take back to the hive and the pollen that has fallen on our bodies…"

"I know… I know this… I know what happens…" said Betsie buzzing into the air with excitement. "Mum says the bees jump from flower to flower and as they do the dust they carry creates new flowers. She must mean pollen dust – which is why without bees we wouldn't have trees and flowers and fruit and…" together they said,

"… and the planet would slowly die…"

"Your mum is right, Betsie. That is exactly why bees are so important," and she puffed herself out with pride. "Come on, Betsie, it's your turn to collect something to take back to the hive. You can take back some nectar or the guard bees won't let you in."

"*Guard bees!*" Betsie said, suddenly sounding worried. "What do you mean the guard bees?"

"Oh, they protect the hive from intruders," Hunnie said, "so you need to drink some nectar to take back to the hive as a gift and then the guard bees will let you in."

Hunnie took off into the sky with the weight of her bulging red pollen baskets pulling her back legs down.

Betsie stayed for a moment on the horse chestnut blossom thinking about what Hunnie had just said about the guard bees. Then with one enormous buzz of her wings she soared into the sky.

"Hunnie!" she said. "Wait for me! What's nectar?"

Chapter 10

LEARNING TO DRINK LIKE A BEE

"Down there!" Hunnie called out. "Look, there's a Mirabelle tree."

Betsie looked down at the trees and there it was, just like the one in her garden, its branches heavy with the prettiest of pale pink blossom.

"Come on," said Hunnie, "you can drink some nectar from the blossoms on that tree…" and she swept down through the air – but Betsie wasn't so quick to follow.

"Just a minute," Betsie said swinging round in front of Hunnie. "What is this nectar that you say I have to drink? If I have to drink something I think I *should know* what it is."

"You are right," said Hunnie gently calming Betsie down. "Let's try and find a space on the Mirabelle tree where there aren't any other bees and I *will* explain."

As they got nearer to the tree Betsie could hear the loud whirring sound of the bees. It reminded her of warm sunny days in May when she would stand underneath the Mirabelle tree in her garden and watch the bees hopping from flower to flower getting on with their work. She would close her eyes and listen to the sound of their wings humming out a tune as they busied themselves. She knew they wouldn't sting her if she stood still because her mother told her honeybees were too busy to want to sting her. Betsie also knew that if a honeybee stings you it dies. Honeybees only use their sting if they feel threatened by something. So Betsie always stood silent and unstirring, under that tree, listening and watching in a *very non-threatening way.* But now here she was with Hunnie, hovering around, until they could find a space to come down, and when they did Hunnie landed on a leaf and Betsie landed on some blossom next to her.

"OK, Betsie…" Hunnie said when they were settled "… honeybees gather nectar from deep inside the blossom," and she looked towards the middle of the Mirabelle blossom. "It's very sweet and sticky." She paused for a moment to think. "We drink it from deep inside the blossom with our tongues that are like straws," and she poked out her tongue. Betsie jumped back and pulled a face. Hunnie pretended not to notice and carried on.

"We store the nectar in our special tummy which is our 'honey tummy' and take it back to the hive to be made into honey."

Betsie frowned. "So when we get back to the hive," she said, "how do we get it *out* of our tummies?"

"Oh, that's simple. We give it to one of the house bees who uses *her* tongue like a straw to take it from us."

Betsie stuck out her tongue, peered down at it and looked up at Hunnie.

"You're a honeybee now, Betsie and I promise it will all feel very normal once you start drinking. Now put your tongue away. Did your mother never tell you it was rude to poke out your tongue?"

Betsie slowly pulled back her tongue and stared solemnly at Hunnie.

"Come on, Betsie. Time to go and fill your tummy with delicious, gooey nectar."

"Oh," said Betsie, a little unsure, and she stumbled around the flower for a second or two. "Here I go then…" and with that she quickly buried her head deep inside the flower before she had any more time to think.

Inside, it looked like a big green cereal bowl and at the bottom of the bowl she could see the sticky nectar. Just as Hunnie had told her, she stuck out her straw-like tongue, and sucked up the nectar.

When she came up for air, Hunnie was anxiously waiting for her.

"How was that, Betsie?"

"Sticky and sweet!" said Betsie, blinking and smiling in the sunlight as she speedily flew to another flower to see if she could drink some more.

Hunnie hovered above her to make sure she didn't lose sight of her. Betsie went from flower to flower feeling her tummy getting fuller and fatter with every drink she took.

"Aren't you full up yet?"

"I am a bit," said Betsie puffing out her tummy. "I'd say I am about ready to burst!"

"Come on then… *let's go.* It's time to go back to the hive," and they took off into the sky.

"Betsie!" Hunnie said. "You're a forager bee!"

"I'm a what?"

"A forager bee."

"What does that mean?" Betsie asked, looking a little worried.

"It means you go out and search for food – you forage for food – a forager bee. Get it?"

"I get it," said Betsie doing loops in the air. "I get it. I am a forager bee. I forage for food." She started spinning around in the air.

"I'm a…" All of a sudden she stopped.

Hunnie turned and went back to find her. Betsie was looking sad and confused.

"Hunnie…" she said, sounding a little bothered, "… does that mean I'm not a honeybee any more?"

"No… you are still a honeybee. It's just a name we give to the bees that go out and bring back the food." Betsie let out a big sigh of relief. She was *still* a honeybee, but not just any old honeybee – a *forager bee!*

"Hurrah! Hooray!" she shouted and off they flew in the direction of the hive.

Chapter 11

LONG LIVE THE QUEEN

"There it is!" Hunnie said, sounding very excited. "That's my hive! The one in the middle."

"Oh!" said Betsie flying as fast as she could to catch up. "I thought bees could go in any hive."

"No! Of course not! That would be like you going into one of your neighbour's houses without asking!"

"But you're a bee… surely *bees* can go in any hive?" said Betsie.

"No!" said Hunnie. "Come on… down we go again."

Betsie followed on behind. They settled down on a lavender bush laden with purple flowers and bursting with the sound of busy bees going about their business.

"It's best you know all this before we get to the hive," Hunnie said, wandering around, taking in the amazing scent of lavender. She found the quietest spot she could and turned and looked at Betsie.

"In each hive," she said, "as I have already told you, there is a queen bee."

Betsie looked at Hunnie and curtsied. Hunnie shook her head and continued.

"And the queen, as I have also told you, is the most important bee in the hive."

"Well, she would be!" said Betsie. "She is the queen after all."

"Quite!" said Hunnie as Betsie buzzed up in the air with excitement at the very thought that she might see the queen. Hunnie waited patiently for Betsie to come back down.

"She is important because, without her, the hive would not survive. She is the only female in the hive who can lay eggs and so provide us with new bees!"

"She lays *all* of the eggs?" Betsie said, sounding surprised.

"Yes. All of them. A good queen will lay two thousand eggs a day. She never stops!"

"Wow," said Betsie, "that's a whole lot of eggs."

"However," Hunnie said, "the queen needs the worker bees in order to survive herself. We clean her and we feed her. We are the ones that bring back the pollen and nectar that feeds *all* the bees in the hive. And, we, the workers, run the hive from the day we are born to the day we die."

"Goodness," said Betsie.

"Every queen bee," Hunnie said, "has a very special aroma. It's like a perfume and it's exclusive to her. It's called a pheromone."

"A phero what?"

"Phero*mone*," said Hunnie. "It's a smell… and that's how we know which hive is ours… *we can smell her!*"

Betsie started to giggle.

"Why are you laughing, Betsie?"

"Oh I'm sorry…" said Betsie trying to stop, "I was just thinking how funny it would be if all the kings and queens in the world had different smells! *Your Majesty…*" Betsie said bowing right down… "*you must be from England… I can tell from your smell!*"

"Being able to smell where *our* queen is, is *very* important to a honeybee," said Hunnie, a little annoyed by Betsie's amusement. "If we couldn't smell her all the bees would start going into the wrong hives, fighting would break out and it would be complete chaos!"

"Am I going to actually meet the queen?"

"Well, you won't exactly meet her," Hunnie said, "she's far too busy and she is always surrounded by her attendants."

"Attendants?" Betsie said.

"Yes, they are the ones who feed and clean her as she walks around. But you will definitely see her because the queen, once mated, never leaves the hive unless she swarms."

"Wow!" said Betsie, wondering what Hunnie meant by '*swarms*', but more interested in the queen *never* going out.

"Why doesn't she ever leave the hive?"

"Because it's too dangerous outside for her and, as I said, we need her to produce new bees so the colony can survive."

"Gosh," Betsie said. "Does she wear a crown?"

"No, she doesn't wear a crown," Hunnie said, laughing at the very thought.

"How will I know she's the queen?"

"Oh, like I told you, she looks very different to all the other bees in the hive," Hunnie said. "She is bigger than all the other bees, not massively bigger, but bigger. She's quite long and slender and…" she paused for a moment, "and *very beautiful*. You will definitely know it is the queen when you see her."

"Will I have to curtsy?" Betsie asked, practising her curtsy whilst mumbling *Your Majesty* under her breath.

"No, Betsie, you won't have to curtsy."

"Oh, that's a shame," said Betsie.

"But you are bringing a gift to her hive, which is very important," said Hunnie.

"Am I?"

"Yes, Betsie. The nectar you have collected, remember?"

"Oh yes! The nectar!" Betsie looked down at her fat tummy bulging with nectar.

"And that's why the guard bees will let you in, because you have a present for the hive!"

"Oh!" Betsie said, suddenly remembering. "The guards… I had forgotten about the guards," and she let out a loud groan.

"They will be fine. Come on, we're nearly there… let's go!"

Hunnie flew up into the air but Betsie stayed on the lavender bush for a moment thinking about the guards. Suddenly her wings felt very heavy, and she didn't seem to be able to lift herself up into the air.

"Come on, Betsie," Hunnie said, not noticing her friend was neither behind nor beside her. "You can't fail now, we're nearly there."

Betsie finally took off but she wasn't laughing and she wasn't doing loops either. In fact, she wasn't so sure being a honeybee was a very good idea right now.

Chapter 12

NOT SO SURE

Hunnie started to swoop down towards her hive and was just about to say something to Betsie when she spotted that she was nowhere to be seen. She stopped and waited until finally Betsie came into view.

For the first time since she became a bee, Betsie wasn't racing or challenging Hunnie as to who could do the most loops in a few seconds and Hunnie noticed that Betsie didn't look very happy at all.

"Betsie! Are you hurt?"

"No," Betsie said as she caught up with her. "I'm just not sure I still want to be a bee."

Hunnie looked shocked and then concerned.

"Why not? What's happened?" she said, hovering and buzzing all around her.

"Well…" Betsie said nervously, "it's the…"

Hunnie watched and waited for Betsie to say what was bothering her.

"It's the… *guards!*" Betsie said very quickly. "There, I've said it. I'm afraid of the guard bees."

"And so you should be," Hunnie said smiling. "They are there to do a very important job. They have to keep robber bees, wasps and any other intruders away from our hive."

Betsie let out a long sigh.

"You mentioned the guards when you said I had to bring something back to the hive but I forgot to ask you who they were. But the very word '*guards*' told me they were there to protect the hive because that's what guards do!" Betsie started to fly backwards. "And, well, I am just not sure about it all now." She turned around and looked back towards her house. Hunnie flew round in front of her.

"Well don't worry," she said. "I wouldn't take you anywhere I thought you might come to harm." Betsie looked at Hunnie, and Hunnie continued in a very reassuring voice.

"That's why you have a present for the hive. The nectar," she said, "they will see you have brought something good to the hive and will let you in."

"Are you *sure?*" Betsie said, desperately needing encouragement.

"I am sure. Come on, follow me, we won't go straight in," Hunnie said and she began to slowly fly nearer to the hive. "We can land on the roof and you can watch the bees going in and out for a while before you enter."

Betsie took another look behind her and then down at the hive below. It really was just a matter of landing on the rooftop now, as Hunnie had gently been guiding them down without Betsie noticing.

"You *will* be fine, Betsie… stay next to me, it's busy down there."

The two little bees landed on top of the roof. They walked to the edge and Betsie looked down.

"Goodness," she said, "look at all those bees!" She could hardly hear herself speak above the bees buzzing to and from the hive.

"I know," said Hunnie, "it's a very warm day and there's a lot to be done on a day like today."

Chapter 13

HALT! WHO GOES THERE?

All of a sudden Betsie heard an intense, piercing buzz. Suddenly, from out of nowhere, a guard bee landed on the roof directly in front of her. Betsie froze and held her breath. She didn't dare even so much as glance at Hunnie. Her heart was thumping so hard she was terrified the guard would hear it. *Please… please… please go away*, she thought as she stared straight ahead. The guard bee touched Betsie with her antennae, then as quickly as she had appeared, she was gone and Betsie let out a huge sigh.

Betsie stayed exactly where she was, rigid with fear. Hunnie rushed across the roof and gently urged Betsie back toward the middle.

"Oh, Hunnie," she said as soon as she could find her voice. "That was awful, hideous, horrid!"

Hunnie looked at her dear friend who was looking very afraid.

"I thought I was going to die!" Betsie said.

"Betsie Valentine," Hunnie said, "I told you, if I thought you were in danger I would not have brought you here. She was just doing her job!"

"I know…" Betsie said with tears of relief welling up in her eyes. "But when she looked at me with those fierce eyes, and that loud buzzing sound she made was so much louder than anything I have ever heard a bee do before, I…" Betsie paused for a moment. "I… well, I have never been so afraid."

"Fierce eyes, you say?" said Hunnie.

"Yes. Angry, fiery, murderous eyes!"

"Loud buzzing?"

"Yes. A powerful, deafening, furious buzz!"

"Like this?" Hunnie said and she flew up into the air and circled around and came back down hovering right in front of Betsie, glaring at her and buzzing her wings loudly.

"Yes," said Betsie walking backward, "like that!" she said really wishing with all her heart she wasn't a bee. "Hunnie, you're scaring me… please stop!"

Hunnie came down onto the roof and gently went and stood next to Betsie.

"Do I look scary now?" Hunnie said nudging her friend so she would turn and look at her.

"No," said Betsie, sounding upset "no... you don't."

"Well," said Hunnie, "I used to be a guard bee."

"You did?" Betsie took a few steps backwards.

"Yes," said Hunnie proudly. "All worker bees have to do guard duty. It's the very last job you have before you become a flying bee and leave the hive." Hunnie walked toward Betsie who was now standing dangerously close to the edge of the back of the roof. "From the moment we are born to the moment we die, there are various jobs we *have* to do and being a guard bee is just one of them."

"So the guards aren't specially trained mean bees?" Betsie said, looking nervously at Hunnie.

"No, Betsie, they are not *specially trained mean bees!* You only think they look scary because they are called *guards*. And yes, because they have a job to do, protecting the hive, their buzz is, let's say, more strident. We don't want robber bees or wasps coming in."

"So the way you looked at me just then…" Betsie said.

"That was my guard face!" Hunnie said and she sprang around and looked at Betsie.

"Halt! Who goes there?" Hunnie said and she started to laugh.

Betsie looked at Hunnie and started to relax.

"However," said Hunnie "you *should* know that a honeybee's sting is at its most venomous when she is guarding the hive, so you really don't want to upset her. But they actually look just like you and me."

Betsie and Hunnie gradually made their way back to the edge of the roof and stood watching all the comings and goings of the hive. Every now and then Betsie looked at Hunnie to make sure she was the honeybee she had come to know and not the guard bee.

The flying bees were walking out of the darkness into the daylight, briefly stopping before they took off into the air. The bees returning to the hive either had their back legs laden with pollen or their special tummies bulging with nectar.

Some of the other bees, Hunnie explained, were returning with water they had collected from little puddles to help thin out the honey in the hive. And some had a gooey substance that they had gathered from plant buds to fill up any cracks that had appeared in or outside of the hive. The guard bees were always in and out checking every bee as it came and went to make sure no one who entered was going to make trouble.

"What are *they* doing?" Betsie asked pointing to a few bees, with their bottoms in the air, vigorously fanning their wings at the entrance to the hive.

"Oh, they are fanning bees," Hunnie said, "they are keeping the hive cool with their wings," and she leaned forward with her bottom pointing toward the sky and fanned her wings as fast as she could.

Betsie spread out her wings and did the same. They looked at each other and laughed then flew around above the rooftop fluttering their wings, cooling each other down and laughing once again!

"Are you ready to go in?" Hunnie said.

"I am," said Betsie, feeling happy and confident at last.

"Well let's go!" said Hunnie and they flew off the roof and went down and joined the other bees as they queued in the air to get into the hive.

Chapter 14

A CLOUD OF BEES

The two little bees hovered side by side, gradually making their way down toward the entrance to the hive. Suddenly, the sky above them became dark and filled with the deafening sound of buzzing bees. Hunnie and Betsie looked up at the sky, which had come alive with thousands of bees all swooshing and swirling around. Betsie stared at Hunnie.

"What's going on?" she said as she started to fly back towards the roof.

"It's a swarm!" Hunnie said shouting above the noise. "The bees from one of the other hives are swarming!"

They landed back on the roof and Betsie looked up at the swarm of bees above her. She had never seen or heard anything like it. It was chaotic. She remembered that Hunnie had mentioned swarming when she was telling her about the queen.

She also remembered her mum talking about *checking the bees to make sure they didn't swarm* but she had never thought about what it meant.

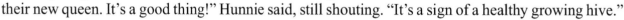

"Why are they doing this?" Betsie said in a loud voice hoping Hunnie could hear her above the commotion.

"A new queen must have been or is about to be born," said Hunnie, "so the old queen has to leave the hive!"

"But there are thousands of bees up there. Are they chasing her away?"

"No!" Hunnie said. "They are the flying bees. She takes them with her so she can start a new colony."

"Gosh!" Betsie looked up again. "There can't be many bees left in that hive."

"There aren't," Hunnie said. "Sometimes as many as half the bees take off with the old queen to find a new home and the young bees that are left behind have to start again with their new queen. It's a good thing!" Hunnie said, still shouting. "It's a sign of a healthy growing hive."

"Goodness!" Betsie said, crouching as low as she could to try and escape the confusion.

"Look, Betsie!" Hunnie said looking at a tree nearby. "The old queen must have flown into that tree!"

Betsie watched as all the bees that had formed the black cloud above them began to fly towards a branch in an old apple tree not far from the hive they had just come out of.

"They are gathering together around the queen to protect her," Hunnie said.

"Will they be OK?" Betsie said, fascinated by what she was seeing.

"Oh yes," Hunnie said. "They have been planning this for some time now."

And just as suddenly as the chaos and noise had started, it stopped. The bees huddled themselves around the old queen and formed into the shape of a rugby ball that hung, humming and fizzing with life, from the branch of the tree.

"They ate lots of honey before they left the hive," Hunnie said, "so they wont be hungry… in fact their tummies are so full of honey, they don't even sting!"

"Is that where they will live now?" Betsie said as she watched the last few bees attach themselves to the cluster.

"No…" Hunnie said, "they will look for somewhere else, this is just their resting place. When they are all settled some of the other bees will go and look for somewhere safer. They are called scout bees because they look around for a place to live."

Betsie felt herself relax as everything calmed down. She was just about ready to fly back down to the entrance when, out of the corner of her eye, she saw a man wearing a bee suit, just like her mum's, walking toward the hives, carrying a large cardboard box.

"Hunnie!" Betsie said. "Someone's coming!"

Hunnie and Betsie watched as the man looked up at the swarm of bees in the tree and he put the box on the ground. Out of the box he took a large white sheet and placed it directly under the swarm. He then placed the box on top of the sheet.

"What's he doing?" Betsie said quietly.

"He's collecting the swarm before the scout bees take them off somewhere else."

"Why?" Betsie said. "Why would he do that?"

"Because," Hunnie said in a sombre voice, "honeybees can't survive in the wild anymore, they have to live in hives or they will die."

"But you said the scout bees would go and look for somewhere *safe* for them to live!"

"I know," said Hunnie "they will… but beekeepers know the bees will die if they are left alone and not put in a hive, which is why they try and get to the swarm before they have a chance to fly off again."

The two bees watched as the man reached into his pocket and took out a pair of secateurs and then stretched up to reach the branch that the bees were hanging on. As skilfully as he could he cut the branch away from the tree and calmly placed it across the box. Then with the greatest of care he gently shook the swarm off the branch. Only a few bees flew up in the air. He peered down into the box and once he was confident that he had the queen and all her flying bees inside, he turned the box over so it was upside down, protecting the swarm inside. He propped one side of the box up with a stone so the flying bees that were left in the tree could smell the queen and come and join her.

"Why will they die if they don't go in a hive?" Betsie said while looking back at the other bees still buzzing around their hives as if nothing had happened.

"Diseases," said Hunnie. "Diseases that have been brought from other countries by other bees. We cannot live without your help now."

"So my mother really is doing a good thing by keeping bees?" Betsie said.

"Yes, Betsie, she is. You need the bees and we need you," Hunnie said nestling up next to her.

"Wow," said Betsie as she looked at her friend. "*We really do need each other.*"

"We do indeed," Hunnie said.

The man started to walk away, leaving the box of bees in the shade.

"What will happen to the box of bees now?" Betsie said, surprised, as she watched the man get in his car.

"Oh, he'll come back when the sun has gone down and the bees have all settled and he'll put them into their new hive. It's fantastic to watch!" Hunnie said.

"Will I be able to see it?"

"Maybe… later," Hunnie said, "but right now, now everything has calmed down, we have our own hive to go into – remember?"

And they flew back up into the air and rejoined the other bees waiting to get into the hive.

Chapter 15

INTO THE DARKNESS

The two little bees hovered side by side, gradually making their way down toward the entrance to the hive.

"By the way, Betsie," Hunnie said above the din of buzzing bees. "Don't forget the guard bees' sting is at its strongest!"

"That's… that's… that's great," Betsie stammered. "Thanks for reminding me, Hunnie."

"You're welcome!" said Hunnie teasingly, adding "… thought you might have forgotten."

And suddenly there they were right in front of the entrance facing the guard bees.

Betsie looked all around her to see what the other bees were doing. It was just like a busy airport, she thought, with all the comings and goings of the bees, and she was finding it hard trying to keep up with Hunnie as she landed on the front of the hive just to the side of the entrance.

"Just keep going," Hunnie said scurrying along, dodging in and out of the other bees while hoping Betsie hadn't noticed a guard bee making her way towards them. But Betsie had noticed and she stopped dead, frozen to the spot, she couldn't help herself. The guard bee walked around Betsie looking her up and down, and Betsie held her breath and stared straight ahead as she had done before. She could see Hunnie carrying on walking without her. She didn't move a muscle as the guard bee touched her with her antennae. Satisfied that she was no threat to the hive, the guard scampered off back to her position. Betsie let out a huge blast of air and dashed off to catch up with Hunnie.

"You said you wouldn't leave me!" Betsie said, feeling disgruntled.

Hunnie reassured Betsie, "I could see you," she said. "If I had stood still the guard would have wondered why and *I knew* she would let you in, and look… here you are… about to go into the hive!"

Betsie's eyes opened wide as she peered into the darkness, forgetting about the guard bees. She could feel herself smiling from the inside out. She walked through the entrance, her eyes gradually adjusting to the lack of light.

Hunnie quickly scurried ahead of her and when they were safely inside she turned around and faced Betsie.

"Welcome…" she said proudly. "Welcome, Betsie Valentine, to my hive!"

"Gosh," Betsie said, feeling her way around, "it's very dark and noisy in here!"

"You'll soon get used to it… in a bee sort of way," Hunnie said cheerily, staying as close to Betsie as she could. She led the way up and along one of the sides of the hive, all the way to the back, weaving her way in and out of the occasional bee with Betsie hot on her tail. When they got to the very back they walked down onto the floor and stopped. It was far less busy here.

"Look up, Betsie," Hunnie said. "What you can see above you are frames."

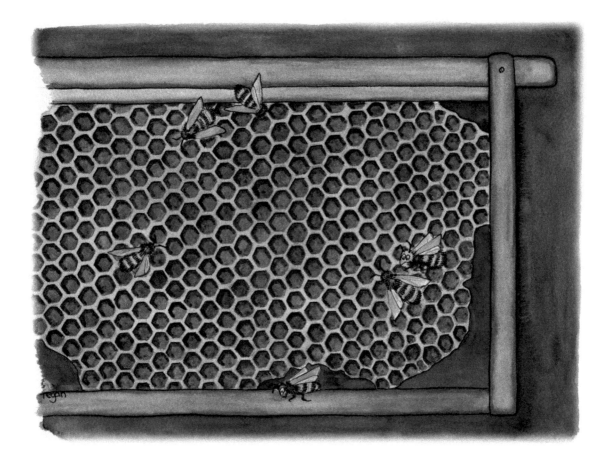

Betsie looked up and hanging just above her was indeed a long oblong-shaped wooden frame with a sheet of golden wax inside.

"There are eleven frames in our hive," Hunnie said, "and the one at the back isn't normally very busy so we can rest here for a moment whilst you *tune in!*"

Betsie blinked a few times and before very long she was seeing like a bee.

"Amazing!" said Betsie as they climbed up onto the sheet of wax. "Where are all the bees?" she said looking at the few that were there. "I can hear them and I can smell them but apart from the odd bee wandering around," she said as one walked past, "I can't see any others."

"Oh you will!" said Hunnie. "As soon as we climb over the top of the frame and go onto the other side, trust me, you will definitely see them."

"The smell is awesome," Betsie said. "It's like honey and wax polish all rolled into one," and she ran toward the top of the frame. "I love it," she said as Hunnie chased after her but Betsie was already at the top. "Oh!" she said coming to an abrupt halt. "*Hunnie!*" she said in a panic. "*Hunnie!*"

"Yes, Betsie. I know," Hunnie said keeping her voice calm and steady. "There are a lot of bees on the other side of the frame. That's what I was trying to tell you."

Betsie's eyes were as wide as wide could be. Bees were everywhere, pushing past her in all directions. There wasn't a single space which wasn't occupied by a bee.

Betsie began to feel a bit wobbly, completely overwhelmed by the incredible sight of all the honeybees busily getting on with their work.

"Hunnie…" she said, "my head's all fluffy and light and my legs…" Betsie began to feel a little unsteady at the top of the frame so Hunnie guided her back down to the other side where it was quiet.

"It's OK, Betsie, it's a lot to take in all at once… *fifty thousand bees*."

"Fi… fif… I can't say it, Hunnie," Betsie said staring at her. "Fifty… thousand… honeybees."

A few bees started coming over to their side of the frame. They walked around in circles, made their way down to the bottom of the hive and then set off towards the entrance. Betsie and Hunnie stood together watching them.

"We'd better start to wander around and try to look a bit busy," Hunnie said, hoping a little walking about would help calm her down. "Look, Betsie…" Hunnie said, quickly changing the subject, "… here comes a drone."

Betsie shook her head. "What?" Betsie said suddenly "A what?"

"A drone!" said Hunnie, looking at a fat bee with big googly eyes.

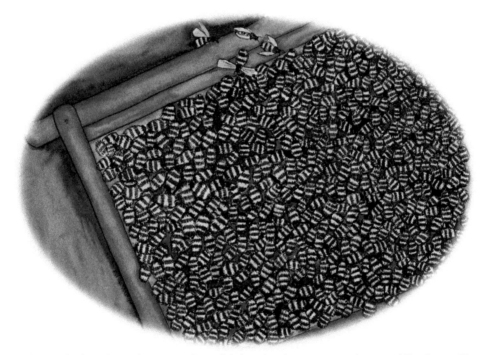

"That's the male bee isn't it?" Betsie said, beginning to sound more like herself again.

"It is," Hunnie said, surprised Betsie had remembered.

"Why's he so fat? He looks like he's eaten all of the honey," Betsie said, giggling.

"Well, yes, actually – he has. Not all of it of course, but a lot of it," Hunnie said with a scowl. "In fact, that's all they do," Hunnie said. "Those that don't manage to mate with the queen come back to the hive and spend the rest of their days eating honey!"

Betsie looked at Hunnie who was watching the drone as he plodded his way slowly across the frame and Hunnie let out a loud groan at the very sight of him as he disappeared in search of more food.

Chapter 16

WHO DOES WHAT

"I thought you said that honeybees worked hard all of the time," Betsie said as another drone appeared on the frame.

"Ah yes… so *we* do," said Hunnie starting to pace around the frame. "*We,* being *the girls*, the worker bees, the foragers, the scouts, the fanning… Oh I could go on… *we* work very hard from the day we are born to the day that we die."

Betsie could see from the way she was walking and talking that Hunnie was getting quite agitated while talking about the drones.

"The queen," Hunnie said, "as I have told you already, works hard from the day *she* is born till the day *she* dies." Betsie bowed her head in respect to the queen. "The queen is the only bee in the colony who has mated and as I told you she spends every waking moment of her days and nights laying eggs. The nurturing of the eggs and the rearing of the young is done by the worker bees. And that leaves…" Hunnie said groaning "… *the drones…*"

"Don't they do *any* work?" Betsie said, still watching the drone.

"No Betsie – they do not!" Hunnie chased the drone away. "They are born, they do nothing," she said walking back towards Betsie. "Admittedly, when they are mature they go out on a warm sunny day and congregate in the air with other drones to mate with a queen, which *is* important." Hunnie tutted. "It's complicated, Betsie," she said. "As soon as the queen goes in amongst them they follow her around in a swarm and it's like a competition to see who can mate with her." Hunnie turned her back, a little concerned about what she was going to tell Betsie next.

"After mating with her, the drones die."

"Oh!" said Betsie sounding alarmed. "That's horrible."

"Those that don't mate with the queen return to the hive and wander around eating honey for the rest of their days."

Betsie looked at Hunnie and back at the drone as he made his way down to the floor of the hive. She felt a bit sorry for him, he looked rather sweet to her.

"They don't even have a sting!" Hunnie said in an exasperated voice.

Not much of a life, Betsie thought, *instant death, after mating with the queen, or a lifetime of being in the way.*

Betsie wandered down to the floor to see if she could see where the drone had gone and Hunnie stood waiting in the middle of the frame. She knew it was just a matter of seconds before Betsie scurried back up. It was very busy down there on the floor and, Hunnie thought, it was about to get a whole lot busier.

Worker bee

Queen bee

Drone

Chapter 17

UP AND OVER

Just as Hunnie had anticipated, Betsie very rapidly came scampering back to her side and stayed as close to her friend as she could.

"It's very busy down there," Betsie said, trying not to look or sound bothered.

"It sure is," said Hunnie, trying not to smile.

Together they walked back over the top of the frame. This time, Betsie hoped, she was a little more prepared for what she was about to see.

"Oh goodness, Hunnie," she said coming to a standstill. "How am I supposed to move around with all these bees? There's no space anywhere."

"It's OK, really it is, you are going to enjoy this bit. Just stick with me," Hunnie said as she made her way across the sticky, syrupy stores of food. "Stick with me," she said again, "do you get it, Betsie? *Stick* with me!" and she looked behind her to see if Betsie was laughing – but she wasn't. She was still standing in the corner of the frame completely overwhelmed by the number of bees and lack of space.

"Come on Betsie, you are a bee… remember? You'll sink in all that gooey honey if you stand there too long," she said, encouraging Betsie to follow her. "All of this honey is the food for the brood," she said suddenly laughing again. "Goodness I am on fire today. Stick with me… food for the brood… that's so funny. My name is Hunnie and I am funny."

Betsie looked at Hunnie and rolled her eyes.

"It's not *that* funny," Betsie said, trying not to smile. "Stick with me… food for the…" her voice trailed off as she clamoured over and navigated her way around the other bees to get to Hunnie.

"And before you ask," Hunnie said, "the brood are all the baby bees." Betsie nodded as they continued to weave their way across the frame.

"What's this?" said Betsie, looking at her feet. They had moved on from the sticky honey and were now walking on a very fine film of white stuff.

"Oh… this is wax," Hunnie said. "Watch the bees and you will see that some of them are filling the cells with the nectar they have collected, ready for it to be turned into honey. Then, once it becomes honey, the others are covering it with a thin layer of wax to protect it. That way it is stored safely for when we need it."

"Wax?" Betsie said. "Where do they get the wax from?"

"Ahhh…" Hunnie said. "Beeswax is made from nectar. When we are about ten days old we develop special glands in our tummies. These glands turn the sugar in the nectar we collect into wax. This wax seeps through our skin and rests on our abdomen and turns into tiny white flakes. It is then taken from us by another bee who chews it until it turns into the wax we are standing on. We use it to build the combs, cap the honey stores and cover and protect the brood."

"Crikey," Betsie said. "That's very complicated and very clever!"

Hunnie bustled with pride and just at that moment she noticed a bee making her way over to

Betsie. The bee stopped and stuck out her straw-like tongue. Betsie quickly glanced over at Hunnie hoping she would tell her what to do.

"Stick your tongue out…" Hunnie said quietly, "… she's a house bee and she wants the nectar you collected."

Betsie drew in her breath.

"I'd forgotten about that!" she said nervously, looking all around her.

"Stick your tongue out, Betsie," Hunnie said again. "Go on."

Betsie poked her tongue out at the bee and closed her eyes. The bee put her straw-like tongue next to Betsie's and began to draw out the nectar. She opened her eyes and watched the bee as she took the very last drop from her tummy. Immediately, Betsie could feel that her special tummy was empty and she put her tongue away. The bee turned around and walked away and Betsie watched her as she put it into a cell.

There!" said Hunnie. "That wasn't so bad, was it?" She beamed at Betsie. "You've given some nectar to the colony, which will now be turned into honey, just like a real honeybee." Betsie looked at Hunnie and felt really proud.

"Awesome," said Betsie. "I am a *real* honeybee. How does the nectar turn into honey, Hunnie?" Betsie said. "Honey… Hunnie," she said again, laughing. "Honey, Hunnie… get it?"

"I get it," said Hunnie. "Trust me, I get it. Now look around you, Betsie" she said. "Can you see some of the bees are fanning their wings just like they did at the entrance?" Betsie looked around the frame.

"Yes," she said. "You told me they were keeping the hive cool."

"That's right. Fanning bees have all sorts of jobs. Some use their wings like fans to keep the queen warm during the winter. In the summer they stand outside the hive and use them to cool it down, and some, like these ones, fan their wings to evaporate the water from the nectar, which then turns into sticky honey."

"Goodness!" said Betsie. "That looks and sounds like hard work."

"It is. It can take several weeks to turn the nectar into honey."

Betsie opened up her wings and looked at them, amazed that these delicate little things could do so many different jobs.

Chapter 18

A RICH TAPESTRY OF COLOUR

Betsie wasn't looking where she was going. She was following Hunnie while watching the bees doing all their different jobs, so she hadn't noticed that they had gone over to another frame. All of a sudden she came to an abrupt halt.

"This is beautiful," she said, gasping as she gazed at the different coloured cells.

"This is pollen," Hunnie said, proudly brushing the pollen she had collected from the back of her legs into an empty cell.

Every cell was filled with different coloured pollen and to Betsie it looked like a rich carpet of endless colours. She turned around in a circle and felt as if she had never seen anything quite so magnificent before.

"Do you remember all the different flowers we talked about?" said Hunnie. "And all the different coloured pollen they produce?"

"Yes," said Betsie hesitantly. "But I don't remember which flowers produce which colour pollen."

"OK," said Hunnie. "You jump onto a pollen cell and call out the colour you are standing on and I will name the flower it came from!"

Betsie immediately jumped onto a cell and shouted out...

"Orange."

"Dandelion," Hunnie said, quick as she could.

"Black."
"Poppy."
"Red."
"Dahlia."
"Purple."
This time Hunnie didn't answer her. She had started to wander away.
"Come on," Hunnie said, "there's a lot more to see… borage, by the way."

Chapter 19

SPOT THE DIFFERENCE

The two bees walked side by side up over onto the next frame. Betsie stood and looked all around her. This frame was very different to the others she had seen. Around the edges of the frame there were the stores neatly covered in a thin layer of white wax. Then there were what looked to Betsie like some empty cells. In the middle of the frame there was a large oval shape of pure golden wax.

"This…" Hunnie said in a gentle whisper, "… is all the brood. Underneath this golden wax carpet, waiting to be born, are all the little worker bees."

Betsie turned cautiously in a circle looking underneath her feet.

"Wow, there's so much. So many little worker bees waiting to be born," Betsie said. "If these are the worker bee brood, where's the drone brood?"

"Look around the edge of the worker brood and you can see some larger lumpy-looking ones," said Hunnie. "Those are the drone cells, they are large and lumpy, like the drones!"

"There aren't very many," Betsie said as she noticed the bigger, bobbly-looking cells.

"No, that's because the hive doesn't need many drones!" Hunnie said. "Like I told you, their only job is to mate with the queen, and those that don't mate with her return to the hive…"

"*… and do nothing but eat the honey!*" they said together.

"Lazy old drones," said Hunnie and she started to search around the frame.

"What are you looking for?" Betsie said.

"I'm looking for something, but I don't think we have any in this hive at the moment."

Betsie followed Hunnie closely as she wandered in and out of the other bees, seemingly looking very hard.

"Sometimes…" she said, "they are very hard to spot, then other times there are lots of them so it's not difficult at all."

"Lots of what?" Betsie said impatiently.

"Queen cells!" Hunnie said. "They are very special cells, much bigger than the worker and drone cells."

Betsie suddenly felt excited when she heard the word queen and joined her friend in her search. This, she felt she had to see!

"Instead of lying flat to the frame," Hunnie said, pushing her way through lots of bees, "it hangs down in a cone shape."

"Wow!" said Betsie. "A special cell just for the queen."

"Oh yes it has to be – the queen is so much bigger than all the other bees so she needs a bigger cell. We feed her special food called royal jelly, which is how she grows so big."

"You said there are sometimes lots of queen cells," Betsie said. "How is that possible if there is just one queen in every hive?"

"Well," said Hunnie, stopping her search. "We sometime build lots of queen cells because we are desperate for a queen. The old queen might have died, stopped laying or swarmed. So we need to make sure we get a healthy queen to replace her."

"What happens to them all when they are born?"

Hunnie grimaced. "As soon as the first queen is born she kills off all the other ones that are still in their cells. *Or,* they fight until the strongest one is the only one left!"

"Good grief," said Betsie "That's harsh."

"It has to be," Hunnie said. "There can only be one queen. It's good I can't find one, Betsie, that means the bees aren't going to swarm… remember? Come on, let's go over to the other side, there's still lots more for you to see."

Betsie followed Hunnie, a little disappointed that she wasn't going to see a queen cell but happy that there wouldn't be any swarming in this hive while she was there!

Chapter 20

A BEE IS BORN

"Betsie!" Hunnie said excitedly. "Look in here. These are the little bee eggs."

Betsie gently leaned over and peered inside what she had thought, while on the previous frame, to be an empty cell.

"I can't see anything," she said, looking back at Hunnie.

"Look a bit harder, they are tiny, they look like teeny weeny bits of white cotton!"

Betsie looked all around the cell again.

"Don't look around the edges of the cell," Hunnie said. "Look at the bottom, right in the middle. The queen always lies right in the middle at the bottom of a cell."

"Oh, I see it. I see it now!" Betsie said eagerly. "Gosh, that's small. I was looking for something that looked like a real egg."

"Well, it is a *real egg*," Hunnie said feeling a bit miffed, "except it's a bee egg which is why it's so small." And she pushed Betsie along a little.

"Look here," she said at another cell, "this is what the egg hatches into after three days." Betsie looked in the cell and jumped backwards.

"Urgh… it looks like a maggot!"

"Well, it's certainly *not* a maggot," Hunnie said, surprised at Betsie's reaction. "It's called a larva and if you watch the nurse bees, you can see them feeding the larvae with honey and pollen."

"Nurse bees?" Betsie said. "You have bees who are nurses in your hive?"

"Yes, of course," said Hunnie. "After a bee is born, her first job is to clean herself and then she immediately cleans out her cell so it is ready for the queen to lay another egg inside it."

"Like I have to clean up my room before I leave it?" Betsie said.

"Exactly. Then when she is about three days old," Hunnie said, "she becomes a *nurse bee* and her job is to look after and feed the larvae with honey, pollen, special bee bread and bee milk until it is ready to be cocooned and covered in the golden wax, where it stays until it's born."

"How long is it from being an egg to being born?" Betsie said looking at the pearly-white c-shaped larvae.

"The worker, queen and drones all take a different amount of time," Hunnie said, pushing Betsie out of the way of the house bees who were sweeping the covered brood with their feet to keep it clean. "The drones, of course, take the longest – twenty-four days. The workers take twenty-one days and the queen is born after sixteen days."

Just then Hunnie spotted two little black antennae sticking out of a covered worker brood cell.

"Look there, Betsie… just in front of you, do you see two tiny antennae sticking out of that cell?"

Betsie stepped forward a little and looked very hard.

"I think so…" she said, glancing back at Hunnie who was eagerly watching.

"Keep looking," Hunnie said, "don't take your eyes away from it."

Betsie stood very still watching the two little black antennae waggling around in the air. She turned to look at Hunnie again and Hunnie told her to turn around and keep looking.

"It takes a while," Hunnie said, "but it's worth the wait."

"What's happening?" Betsie said, a little impatiently.

"You'll see, Betsie," Hunnie said softly, telling her to stay quiet and watch.

After a few moments it looked as if something appeared to be chewing its way all around the top of the cell in a perfect circle. Slowly but surely the top of the cell was opened like the lid of a tin can. Bit by bit, with enormous effort, a furry little head appeared and pushed and pushed her way out of the cell. The little baby worker bee emerged triumphantly and staggered about looking at the empty cells immediately around her. She then walked back to her own cell and immediately started to clean it out – just as Hunnie had said she would.

"Wow…" said Betsie. "I have just watched a baby bee being born."

Hunnie looked on with pride.

Betsie shook her head. "Goodness," she said in disbelief. "I never thought I would see *so much* in one day." Betsie felt really touched by the whole experience.

Hunnie softly pushed her along and said cheerfully, "Come on you… we are going up."

"Going up?" Betsie said, wondering what Hunnie meant.

"Yes, Betsie, we are going up!"

Chapter 21

A ROYAL ENCOUNTER

As Betsie followed on behind Hunnie, zigzagging her way between the bees up towards the top of the brood box, she suddenly noticed a circle of bees sweeping their way across the frame.

"Hunnie!" she said, wondering what was coming towards them. "What's going on?"

"That's the queen…" Hunnie said quietly, "… with all her helpers. Stay still and you will see her right in the middle of the circle."

Betsie drew in her breath and didn't dare blink just in case she missed anything. They were moving quite rapidly and it was quite a sight to behold. Hunnie, Betsie and the nurse bees all stepped aside making way for the queen and her attendants to pass through. As they got to Hunnie and Betsie the circle of bees stopped. Betsie looked on in wonder as the queen looked around at her attendants and stretched out her long straw-like tongue towards the nearest one. The little bee dutifully gave her some food, and the queen turned to the next bee, who did the same, and then the next. She carried on until she was satisfied, then as quickly as they had appeared they disappeared… underneath the frame onto the other side where she carried on with the job of laying eggs.

She was just as Hunnie had described, larger than all the other bees, which made her wings look small – with a long, slender, shiny brown body covered in a fine dusting of barely visible golden hairs.

Betsie was left feeling quite overwhelmed. She thought of her mother who would often say, after a hive inspection, that she didn't see the queen. She knew she was there because of all the eggs but she didn't manage to find her. Betsie knew she had just witnessed something very special.

"That was amazing…" Betsie said, "… awesome. That was… I saw the queen… Hunnie… I actually saw the queen!"

"I said you would," Hunnie said with enormous pride. "I knew you would, she's exquisite isn't she?"

"She certainly is," Betsie said, still in wonder at what she had just witnessed. "Oh Hunnie," she said taking a step back, "I saw the queen."

Hunnie looked at her friend, knowing there was still so much more to see, but she let her stand for a moment or two so she could take it all in. The birth of a bee and the queen all in a matter of minutes, it was a lot to take on board.

Betsie felt a gentle nudge and she turned to look at Hunnie.

"We're going up, remember?" said Hunnie.

"Oh yes," said Betsie. "What's going up?"

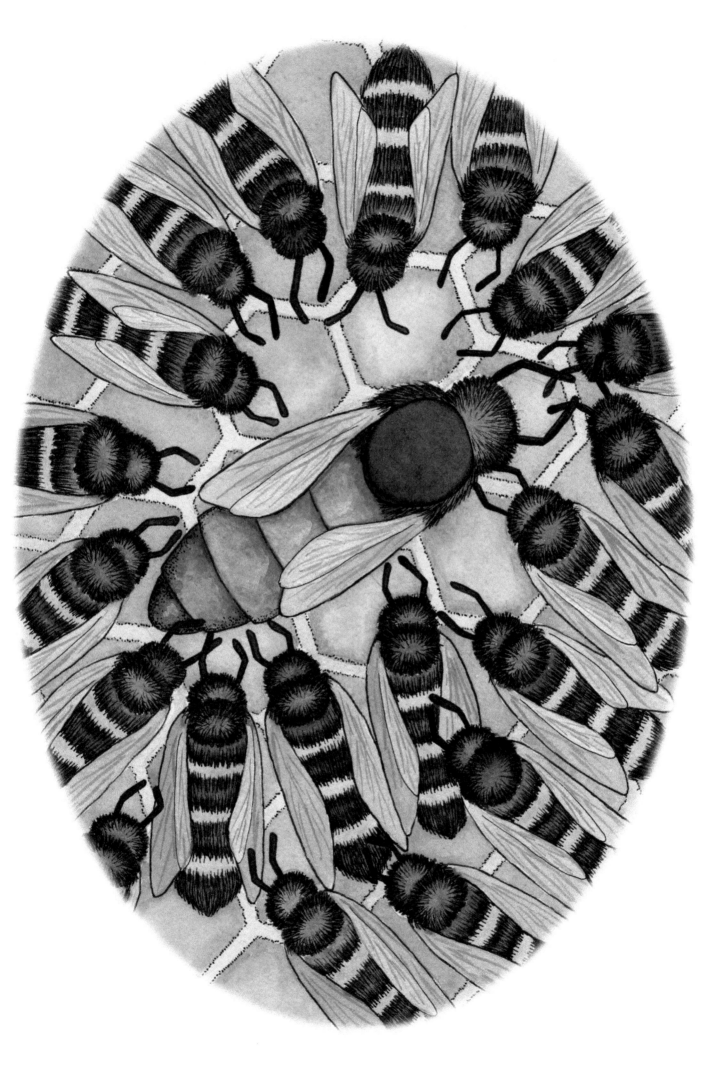

Chapter 22

HONEY! HONEY!

"Where are we going?" Betsie said as she chased after Hunnie. They went underneath the frame and up the other side towards the top of the brood box.

"We are going into the super," Hunnie said. "Right now we are in the 'brood box' where all the young are born and up there is the 'super'. It's just as busy up there as it is down here."

"The super…" Betsie said, "… what's the super?" Hunnie scurried along with Betsie close behind weaving her way in and out of the other bees.

"The super," said Hunnie, "is where we store all our food for the winter. You'll like it up there!"

When they got to the top of the box they came to a halt. There, just above them, was a metal grid that separated the brood box from the super.

"Oh!" Betsie said with a start. "We…" and she was just about to say *'we can't go any further'* when she noticed lots of bees nipping up and down through the small gaps. "Why is this here?" she said.

"This is the queen excluder," Hunnie said. "It's here to stop the queen going up into the super and laying eggs! She is bigger than us so she can't get through the grid. It also stops the dopey drones from eating any more of our honey as they are *too fat* to get through."

"So are we allowed up there?"

"Yes, of course, that's what I meant by *'We're going up!'*" Hunnie said. And with that she popped through the grid, into the super.

"Be careful," Hunnie said to Betsie as she made her way into the super. "It's very sticky up here… there's nothing but delicious golden honey."

Betsie stood watching all the activity going on around her. She noticed the frames were smaller than the ones down below in the brood box. They were just as wide but not quite as deep and the sweet smell of honey was everywhere. The honeybees carried on with their business as always, too preoccupied to notice Betsie. Some were pulling out the wax to build honeycomb for the nectar to be put in and others were covering the filled comb with a thin layer of wax to protect it. *They really do work hard*, Betsie thought, *they never stop.*

"Look Betsie," said Hunnie, turning in the direction of a group of bees. "Here comes a house bee, like the one that took the nectar from you. She is coming in with all the nectar in *her* special tummy." Betsie watched as the little bee came up through the grid and scuttled over to one of the other bees who then put out her tongue, just as Betsie had done, and she took the nectar from the house bee and placed it into the pulled-out comb ready for it to be turned into honey.

"Why is she called a house bee?" Betsie said.

"Because she isn't a flying bee yet, so she stays in the hive, hence she is called a house bee. She stays in the *house*," said Hunnie.

"So the flying bees come into the hive," said Betsie, "and give whatever they have collected to the house bees who then take it to wherever it is needed."

"Yes!" Hunnie said and she turned in a circle with excitement. "The house bee either stores the nectar she has taken from the flying bee in the brood box to be fed to the brood, or she brings it up to the super to be stored for the winter." She was so pleased that Betsie understood.

Together they walked up and over the frames. All the while, Betsie was watching and learning as much as she could. Some of the frames were covered in a thin white layer of wax. The ones that hadn't been covered were filled to the top with bright, glistening, golden honey waiting to be covered with the wax.

Betsie recognised the frames covered with the thin layer of wax. These were just like the ones her mum brought back to the house from her hives in the early summer. She would remove the wax from the frames and spin the frames in a special spinner. Then she would strain it all through a large sieve into a very large plastic bucket with a tap on the side and cover it with a lid. After a day or two she would then transfer all the honey into jars and stick labels on them before she either sold them or gave them away as gifts to family and friends. Everyone loved her mum's honey!

Betsie smiled to herself and closed her eyes and breathed in the balmy scent of sweet honey. *I will never forget this… not ever*, she thought.

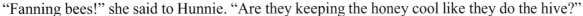

Just then, Betsie noticed some bees with their bottoms in the air, beating their wings very fast over the open honeycomb.

"Fanning bees!" she said to Hunnie. "Are they keeping the honey cool like they do the hive?"

"They are fanning their wings to reduce the amount of water in the nectar. The nectar we bring back from the flowers is about eighty per cent water. The bees fan their wings until it has reduced to about twenty per cent, which is what makes it so sticky. It can take a couple of days." Hunnie paused for a moment and Betsie shook her head in wonder as she watched the fanning bees tirelessly working away.

"When it's nice and syrupy," Hunnie said, "the house bees cover the honey with a thin layer of wax, ready for the winter, so they have something to eat when they can't leave the hive."

"Clever, clever bees," said Betsie. "Oh Hunnie… it's beautiful up here. I could live up here forever. It smells heavenly. Such clever, clever bees!"

"You sound like a drone. Never wanting to do anything except eat all the honey," and she looked at Betsie with great satisfaction. "It does look delicious though!" Hunnie said as she started to walk back down toward the queen excluder.

"It sure does," said Betsie as she made her way back down into the brood box. "It sure does," she said again.

Chapter 23

SHALL WE DANCE?

"We need to head back home soon," Hunnie said, gradually making her way towards the entrance. Betsie stopped. She slowly and deliberately turned in a circle taking in as much as she could. She felt sad at the thought of leaving the hive especially as it all now seemed so familiar to her. The bees, as always, were just getting on with whatever it was they had to do.

The flying bees were coming and going, bringing in the nectar and pollen for food and water to cool everything down. The nurse bees were tending the young. The house bees were taking the nectar from the flying/forager bees. The fanning bees were doing what fanning bees do! She caught a glimpse of the guard bees as they stood at the entrance buzzing loudly.

Betsie walked slowly, in no great hurry to catch up with Hunnie who, it seemed to her, was marching on ahead. To think she had been so frightened when she first arrived and now it seemed, well… normal. Just then, when she thought there could not be anything else to see, she spotted something that didn't look at all familiar or normal. A forager bee was clinging onto the side of the hive while a house bee was struggling to take something, which definitely wasn't pollen, from her legs.

"What's going on there?" Betsie said. Hunnie turned around to look.

"Oh," she said, "that bee has brought back some propolis."

Betsie looked at Hunnie and then back at the two bees who looked as if they were playing a game of tug of war.

"*Propolis*," Hunnie said, "is extremely sticky stuff which we collect from the buds of trees. It's even stickier than honey. It can take two days to take propolis from a bee."

Two days, Betsie thought. *Two days just to have the propolis taken from you.* She let out a long sigh. Going to school, she thought, was beginning to look easy.

"What do you need propolis for?" Betsie said, wincing at the sight of the bees tugging away.

"Ah well," said Hunnie, "it has many uses." And she began to list all the useful things you could do with propolis. "Block up holes, mend cracks, repair comb, make the entrance watertight, cover up things we don't like being in the hive but are too big to move out. It's very handy," she said and they carried on walking when Hunnie saw a bee doing a little dance.

"Betsie, look over there!" she said. A little bee was waggling her bottom, fluttering her wings and moving around in a strange sort of circle.

"It looks as if that bee is dancing," Betsie said. "*Is* she dancing?"

"She is," said Hunnie. "She's doing a *waggle dance*."

Betsie had never seen anything like it.

"What's a waggle dance?" Betsie said, starting to waggle her bottom and flutter her wings.

"Well," Hunnie said, "she's just flown into the hive and is telling the other bees where the flowers are. Look… they are watching her."

"How do they know what she is saying?"

"If you watch her, she is dancing in a figure of eight. If she goes up the middle to the left then that means the flowers are to the left of the sun," said Hunnie, "and if she goes up the middle to the right, that means the flowers are to the right of the sun."

Betsie started to prance up and down copying the bees as they danced.

"I wouldn't do that," Hunnie said "you might confuse all the bees and send them off in the wrong direction!"

Betsie stopped immediately, not wanting to upset the bees and so they carried on.

Hunnie looked at her friend and couldn't resist giving her bottom a little wiggle and Betsie briefly quivered her wings. The two of them turned in a small circle and continued on their way to the entrance.

"Oh Hunnie," Betsie said, "I've had such a great time, I really have and I have learned *so* much about the bees."

Chapter 24

TO SUM UP

"What have you learned about being a honeybee?" Hunnie said, looking at Betsie as they made their way onto the very first frame in the hive – almost back where they had started.

Betsie stood still and thought for a moment. The sound of the buzzing was ringing in her ears. It made it very difficult to think.

"Well," she said, trying very hard to remember *everything*. "I've learned that after you are born you clean out your cell and the other cells around you." Hunnie nodded and Betsie took a deep breath. "Then you become a nurse bee and look after the brood and feed the larvae. After that you become a house bee and you are in charge of building the comb, carrying the food and fanning the hive to keep the temperature steady and reduce the water in the nectar so it turns into honey."

Betsie became distracted when she saw a house bee rolling another bee out of the entrance to the hive.

"That's an undertaker bee," said Hunnie. "They remove the sick and dead bees from the hive."

"Oh! I wouldn't like that job," Betsie said looking shocked. "I wouldn't like that job at all!"

"Well, it has to be done," Hunnie said. "We need all the space we can get and as you now know, Betsie, we don't have choices, we just have duties! Every bee has to do each and every job before she can be a flying bee, so now you can add undertaker bee to the list of jobs."

Betsie continued. "After you are an undertaker bee," Betsie grimaced, "you become a guard bee."

"Oh Betsie," said Hunnie interrupting, "you really have learned so much!" And she felt so happy and proud that her friend now understood exactly how hard a honeybee works and exactly what they have to do to make honey and help keep the planet alive.

The two bees stood looking at each other. They were so very near the entrance now and soon would be flying back to Betsie's house in no time at all. They slowly walked down onto the floor of the hive and towards the soft light streaming in through the opening.

"There's only one job left that you haven't mentioned," said Hunnie, moving as close as she could to Betsie. The two little bees stood beside each other, with their backs to darkness and the gentle sunlight of the late afternoon on their faces.

Betsie looked at all the flying bees that were still busy coming and going, being checked in and out by the guards. She wasn't afraid any more, not one little bit. She looked behind her, back into the darkness and smiled to herself. She had loved being a bee and didn't want to leave the hive. Hunnie looked at her, and nudged her.

"Well?" Hunnie said. "One last job?"

"Oh…" said Betsie, "yes… one more job, the last job a bee has…" she looked at her wings and then back at Hunnie, "… a flying bee…" she said quietly.

"Yes, a flying bee," said Hunnie, looking at Betsie's sad little face.

"The very last job a honeybee has." Betsie looked down. She thought if she looked at Hunnie she might cry.

"Well?" said Hunnie, giving Betsie a big nudge. "Shall we fly?"

The two of them walked out of the hive, into the quiet sunset. By now there was just the occasional bee arriving home after a hard day's work before the sun went down.

Betsie took one last look around her and before she could say *propolis*… Hunnie took off into the air.

Chapter 25

ONE LAST THING

"Look! Over there! The man in the bee suit is coming back," Betsie said as she rushed to catch up with Hunnie.

"You *have* to see this before we go," said Hunnie turning around in the air. "It's fantastic."

The two of them came down on a branch in a nearby tree and watched as the man gently lifted up the edge of the box and looked inside. The swarm of bees were huddled together in the shape of a pear drop at the top of the box in the corner. They had clustered around the queen to keep her safe and warm. He very carefully gathered up the sheet, wrapping it around the box and slowly walked over to a new empty hive. Mindful of not upsetting the bees, he put the box down on the grass and placed a long plank of wood from the entrance of the new hive down to the ground. Betsie looked at Hunnie, wondering what was going on.

"Shhhhhh," said Hunnie, "watch."

The man quietly and calmly picked up the sheet with the box inside and set it down on the plank. He then spread out the sheet, as evenly as he could, so it reached up to the entrance of the hive and all the way down the plank to the grass. He very steadily lifted up the box with all the bees in it and held it just above the sheet. Betsie held her breath. Suddenly he *banged* on top of the box with one of his hands and all the bees fell out at once in a clump on to the sheet. Betsie let out a gasp.

"What?" she said looking at Hunnie and then back at all the bees. Some of them flew up into the air. "What is going on?" she said.

"Watch!" said Hunnie again. "Don't take your eyes off the bees on the sheet."

The bees were making a loud buzzing sound as they scrambled all over each other. *It is chaos*, Betsie thought.

"Look – look – look..." Hunnie said, "... look at the top of the bundle of bees."

Betsie watched as one of the bees walked, all alone, up to the entrance of the hive. It stopped for a second then walked in. *That must be one of the scout bees*, Betsie thought. The bee came out, flew up into the air and back down again. A couple of other bees joined her. They went in and out a few times and then, as if by magic, all the other bees, in a huge mass, started to march up towards the entrance. Betsie could not believe what she was seeing. Eventually, every single bee walked up along the sheet and into the hive.

"That's incredible," Betsie said. "How do they know what to do?"

"It's getting late and it's starting to get cold so they need somewhere to rest overnight, so the scout bees have told them this is a good place."

"Wow!" Betsie said, letting out a long sigh. "Will they stay in there now?" she asked.

"Oh yes," Hunnie said. "I should think so. When the sun comes out tomorrow morning they will have a look around, they'll know they are somewhere safe and start about their business as usual."

Betsie shook her head in amazement. "Clever, clever bees," she said again.

"Talking of which," Hunnie said, taking off into the sky, "this clever bee needs to get you home before it gets too cold for *her* to fly back to her hive."

Chapter 26

HOMEWARD BOUND

Betsie looked back at the hives as they began their journey home. A few of the bees from the swarm were flying about, checking out their new place. She was so sad to be leaving and her wings felt heavy. She was picturing, in her mind, all the different bees doing all their different jobs. *I will NEVER forget this day*, she thought, **never ever**, and she darted through the air and caught up with Hunnie. *What a day! What a fantastic day!* She couldn't wait to tell her mum, and for that matter, Mrs Noyle! She decided she would go round the next day and teach her everything she had learned and hopefully she would listen to her.

Suddenly she felt as if her whole body was smiling from the tip of her antennae to the sting in her tail.

"Come on," Hunnie said. "I'll race you."

And the two little bees zoomed along, swirling in circles, dipping and diving all the way.

Slowly, without Betsie noticing, they started to come down lower and lower. Betsie looked beneath her. She could see her garden and she looked over at Hunnie.

"We're nearly there," Hunnie said.

"I've enjoyed myself," said Betsie cheerfully, "I really have."

"So have I. It's been mad and it's been fun. Come on… one last flower," Hunnie said and the two of them came down together onto a large bright white daisy with a huge yellow centre.

They sat talking about the day, remembering all the things they had seen and done. Starting with Betsie giving Hunnie a name. How scared Betsie had been of the guards. The swarm. How Hunnie had made her jump when she put on her meanest guard face. Betsie waggled her bottom, fluttered her wings and walked around in a figure of eight shouting, 'The sun's over there! It's over there… that way!' And with that they started laughing and fell over right in the middle of the daisy. When they stood up they were covered in bright yellow pollen and they laughed again. They danced all around the daisy, they could not have been happier.

Just then… a large black shadow appeared over the top of their heads. They moved in closer together, stood very still and looked up. A big black round circle was hovering just above them and they could see their reflections in the glass. They heard a loud *click* and the circle disappeared. Betsie took a large breath in and looked at Hunnie.

"That was my mother," she said, her heart pounding with fear.

"What was she doing?" Hunnie said, trying to calm herself down.

"She was taking a photograph of us."

"A what?"

"A photograph," Betsie said. "A picture."

Betsie looked at the expression on Hunnie's face and decided there wasn't enough time to explain what a photograph was.

"You'll just have to come back one day and I will show you how we live and what we do."

"That's a great idea," Hunnie said, looking at her dear friend and smiling. But her smile slowly started to fade as she stood opposite Betsie.

"There's something I haven't told you," she said solemnly. "Honeybees only live for about six weeks in the height of the summer. Five of those weeks we live in the hive and the very last week we become flying bees. We only fly for about a week or so collecting all the pollen and stuff for the hive, and then… well… we die. So I won't be able to come back."

"Oh Hunnie," Betsie said. "I didn't know. I didn't realise. I mean. Oh Hunnie."

"I really do have to go now, Betsie," she said in a gentle voice. "It's getting late and it's starting to get cold… I'll take you back to your honey sandwich."

The two honeybees gently took off together for the very last time. Once again, they flew side by side, this time neither of them saying a word.

Chapter 27

CLOSE YOUR EYES

Betsie came down softly onto her sandwich and Hunnie hovered just a little way above her in the air. She didn't come down. She didn't want to make saying goodbye any more difficult than it already was.

"Well…" said Hunnie, "I guess this is it."

"I guess it is…" Betsie said quietly, and she felt a single tear in the corner of her eye.

"Don't cry, Betsie. It's been such a lovely day, please don't cry. I will never cry when I think about you," Hunnie said. "I will only ever smile. Promise me you'll do the same… please."

Betsie looked down and the little tear fell onto her sandwich. She took a deep breath and closed both eyes and then looked back up at Hunnie, holding back any more tears she felt welling up inside.

"I promise you… I promise I won't cry."

"Close your eyes, Betsie Valentine," Hunnie whispered, "and say your little rhyme."

Betsie gently shut her eyes and Hunnie quietly began to go higher into the air.

"Are you looking at me, little bee?" Betsie said in a tired voice – and she yawned. "Are you looking at me? My name is…

Chapter 28

WAKE UP BETSIE!

"*Betsie!* Betsie Valentine… wake up!" Betsie woke with a start and looked at Mum who was kneeling down beside her. "You haven't finished your sandwich," Mum said, "it's gone all hard in the sunshine."

Betsie rubbed her eyes and looked all around her and then back at her honey sandwich.

"I…" Betsie said looking confused "I…"

"You've been asleep," Mum said softly.

Betsie frowned, leant forward and picked up what was left of her sandwich. It had gone slightly crusty in the sunshine. She turned it around in her fingers. *I haven't been asleep,* she wanted to say, *I've been a honeybee,* but something made her stop.

"Asleep?" she said as she stretched out her arms and yawned.

"Yes," said Mum.

"I had a funny dream then," she said, looking at Tid who was still sitting on the table staring straight back at her.

"I was a… bee."

"A honeybee?" Mum said, with an affectionate laugh.

"Yes…" Betsie said, scooping Tid up off the table, "a beautiful honeybee." And she stood up, holding Tid dangling by one arm, and spread both her arms out wide and made a familiar buzzing sound, like a bee, and started to say her rhyme as she ran towards the kitchen…

61

But she didn't finish it… she sat Tid on the kitchen table.

"Was it a dream?" she asked Tid. "I don't think it was…"

"Betsie," Mum said as she walked into the kitchen, "go and put your shoes on, we're going round to Grandma Belle's for tea."

Betsie ran upstairs and fetched her shoes from her bedroom. She made her way to the top of the stairs and then proceeded to jump down each one until she got to the bottom where she sat down and put on her shoes.

Betsie looked over at Mum who was sitting in the hall looking at some photographs on her computer.

"Jimmie," Mum said, "come here… look at this picture… look at these two little honeybees. Aren't they sweet?"

"Did you take that?" Dad said as he walked toward the computer carrying young Hewey on his hip.

"Yes… just now in the garden. These two little bees were on this large ox-eye daisy and they just seemed to look up at me, they didn't move and I went *click*!"

Betsie looked up and held her breath.

"You should enter that into a competition," Dad said.

Betsie waited until Mum and Dad walked away. Slowly, she stood up from the stair and quietly walked over to the computer. There before her eyes was a picture of her and Hunnie standing in the middle of the daisy, looking up at the camera. It was there as plain as plain could be. *It wasn't a dream*, she thought. **It wasn't a dream.**

"Come on, Betsie!" Mum called out as she waited at the front door. Betsie turned around from the computer, ran past her mum and out of the door toward the car singing…

Are you looking at me, little bee?
Are you looking at me?
My name is Betsie Valentine
And that begins with a B

Are you looking at me, little bee?
Are you looking at me?
My name is Betsie Valentine
And I <u>know</u> I've been a bee!

Betsie climbed into
the car and sat next to Hewey.
She poked him gently in the tummy.
She smiled, opened her eyes as
wide as could be and said,
"*Bzzzzzzzzzz*"